TODAY IS NOT A GOOD DAY FOR WAR

TODAY IS NOT
A GOOD DAY
FOR WAR

David Krieger

Peace —

[signature]

Capra Press
Memorable books since 1969
Santa Barbara

A Robert Bason Book
Published by Capra Press
155 Canon View Road
Santa Barbara, CA 93108
(805) 969-0203
www.caprapress.com

Cover by Samer Mina
Cover photo by Karen Beard/Getty Images
Book design by Kathleen Baushke
Body type is Haarlemmer

Krieger, David.
    Today is not a good day for war / David Krieger.-- 1st ed.
        p.   cm.
    "A Robert Bason book"--T.p. verso.
    ISBN 1-59266-050-9 (trade pbk.) -- ISBN 1-59266-051-7 (lettered)
    1. Peace movements--Poetry. 2. Peace--Poetry. I. Title.

PS3611.R543T63 2005
811'.6--dc22

                                    2004024552

Edition: 10   9   8   7   6   5   4   3   2   1

First Edition

Hibakusha are the survivors of the atomic bombings
of Hiroshima and Nagasaki.
They are ambassadors of the Nuclear Age.
This book is dedicated to them.

ALSO BY DAVID KRIEGER

Peace 100 Ideas (with Joshua Chen)

Hope in a Dark Time, Reflections on Humanity's Future (Editor)

The Poetry of Peace (Editor)

Choose Hope, Your Role in Waging Peace in the Nuclear Age (with Daisaku Ikeda)

Nuclear Weapons and the World Court (with Ved Nanda)

A Maginot Line in the Sky, International Perspectives on Ballistic Missile Defense (Editor, with Carah Ong)

Waging Peace in the Nuclear Age, Ideas for Action (Editor, with Frank Kelly)

Waging Peace II, Vision and Hope for the 21st Century (Editor, with Frank Kelly)

The Tides of Change, Peace, Pollution and Potential of the Oceans (Editor, with Elisabeth Mann Borgese)

PEACE IS . . .

More than the absence of war

The global architecture of human decency

Putting the planet ahead of profit

Basic security for all

Freedom from oppression

Recognition of human dignity

     theirs as well as ours

Everyone's inalienable right

Living gently on the earth

The courage of nonviolence

A process, not an end

A thousand cranes in flight

A gift to children everywhere

Here then, is the problem which we present to you,

stark and dreadful and inescapable:

Shall we put an end to the human race;

or shall mankind renounce war?

–Russell-Einstein Manifesto, July 9, 1955

CONTENTS

TODAY IS NOT A GOOD DAY FOR WAR

HIROSHIMA DREAMS

The night before the city was devastated
By America's new *weapon*
Hiroshima was filled with meandering dreams—

Dreams of every sort.
Strange, awkward dreams, fearful
And feverish dreams—

Deep dreams filled with childish wonder.
Dreams of love and sacrifice, dreams
That took one's breath away—

Recurring dreams and new ones.
Dreams of exquisite beauty
That weighed upon the heart—

Dreams filled with immeasurable grief.
Yet still less than morning would bring.
Do dreams die with the child?

And what of the dreams of mothers
When they are suddenly incinerated?
Are these dreams lost forever?

WAR IS TOO EASY

If politicians had to fight the wars
they would find another way.

Peace is not easy, they say.
But it is war that is too easy—

too easy to turn a profit, too easy
to believe there is no choice,

too easy to sacrifice
someone else's children.

Someday it will not be this way.
Someday we will teach our children

that they must not kill,
that they must have the courage

to live peace, to stand firmly
for justice, to say no to war.

Until we teach our children peace,
each generation will have its wars,

will find its own ways
to believe in them.

REFUGEE EYES

Her eyes penetrate the skin.
They have seen the far side of mountains
and endless desert.
They know what is true.

Her eyes are dark and precise,
lenses on a frightened world—
a world of lust and childish promise.

Her eyes are at home in the sea,
in clear Caribbean waters.
In the frozen chill of the Arctic
they read stars like an ancient poem.

Before her gaze
steel softens and diamonds shatter.
The world floats slowly away.

THE YOUNG MEN WITH THE GUNS

for Father Roy Bourgeois

"Let those who have a voice speak for the voiceless."
–Bishop Oscar Romero

None of it could have happened,
not the killings, the rapes, the brutality,
without the young men with the guns.

Bishop Romero saw this clearly.
Lay down your arms, he said.
This, the day before his assassination,

the day before they shot him at the altar.
God, forgive them, they only follow orders.
They know not what they do.

But the politicians and the generals
know what they do
when they give their orders
to murder at the altar.

None of it could have happened
not the killings, the rapes, the brutality
without the politicians and the generals,

the ones who sit in dark rooms
and stuff their mouths with food
before they give the orders.

The people are silent.
Their mouths will not open.
They hang their heads and avert their eyes.

Of course, they are afraid
of the young men with the guns
who carry out the orders.

None of it could have happened
without the people remaining silent.

The Bishop staggered, he bled, he died.
But he will never be silenced.

FOUR BRONZE FIGURES
WITHOUT HEADS

The mourners sit
at a right angle
to the four headless
bronze figures.

A bright young cellist,
a favorite
of the man who died,
plays Bach.

I turn and gaze
at the headless figures.
Dappled afternoon light
softens them.

A small bird settles,
and flutters its wings
where a head might have been.

From what unspeakable place
did they so recently arise?
And where are they going
with such motionless resolve?

SPRING MORNING

Last night
dark clocks
sprung ahead
and now
I lie in bed
listening
to the crow
of cocks
the clucking
of hens
the call
of small
birds
the ring
of shots
from far off
wars.

Oak leaves
stir.
I watch
the play
of light
in a prism.
Women
in dark shawls
pray
lava flows
young men
sink in sweet earth.

IN MY ANGER

in my anger
i denounced
punctuation
down with
arrogant periods
and smug commas
death to the fat
capitals

unable though
to carve out apostrophes
i simply accepted
their occasional presence
among my words

with colons it was different
these i grew to love
perpendicular breasts:
uniting space with space

DACHAU

This plain unremarkable place
with its simple buildings and wooden bunks
speaks of fear,
speaks in unspeakable silence
of what occurred here,
when arrogance unleashed
a steady flood of violence
and men were treated as numbers.

This flat gray place,
with its electric barbed-wire fences
speaks of failure,
speaks of evil and brutality
beyond our normal senses.
This place speaks of barren hearts
and hatred, of cold numbness
day after day after day.

This place, with its black iron gate
that says, "Work sets you free,"
speaks of courage
against the power of the state,
when the simple act of living
was a victory.
This place speaks of numbered heroes
who had the cause,
but never lost their souls.

ALL OF THIS

We have made words
into dangerous weapons,

lived in darkness
and slowly emerged.

We have found shadows
where none were lost

and hunted wisdom,
always tracking upwind.

We have sought beauty
to fill empty spaces,

seen our reflections
in a thousand rivers.

We have hinged the sky
and swung it open.

In a moment's dream
we have done all this.

EMPTY SUDDENLY

Her man is gone, and she's alone.
He's gone and buried and done.
She can't forget her man is gone
because he's not ever coming back.

He's gone every minute.

When the hurting stops,
then maybe he'll be gone.
But the shrapnel from the Claymore mine
is all around.

MADMEN

The world is ruled by madmen—
Mad George, mad Saddam,
Mad Tsars, Kings and Emirs,
Mad Generals, Presidents,
Queens and Prime Ministers.

Children, listen to them carefully.
For you, they do not give a damn
And they will use your heads
For battering rams—these madmen,
Mad George, mad Saddam.

A SHORT HISTORY LESSON: 1945

August 6th:
Dropped atomic bomb
on civilians
at Hiroshima.

August 8th:
Agreed to hold
war crimes trials
for Nazis.

August 9th:
Dropped atomic bomb
on civilians
at Nagasaki.

JULY 16, 1945

The Nuclear Age was born
on the broad plains of America,
a land of civility and arrogance.
Born of fire dream and childish exuberance,
its mother was fear; its father, genius.

When the mushroom cloud rose in the sky
Hitler was already dead, the war in Europe ended.
Still, the scientists who watched
cheered like schoolboys.
The victory was theirs.
They had exploded matter
and imploded intellect.

Soon Hiroshima, soon Nagasaki.
Soon the Great Potlatch.

HIROSHIMA, AUGUST 6, 1945

It was a clear sky.
The air tingled with heat and promise,
        that morning in Hiroshima
as men and women set off for work
and children kissed their mothers goodbye.

As the bomb drifted toward earth
city people walked with small steps
        along narrow roads
        across graceful bridges
not knowing they were
        on their way
                to oblivion.

The shadow of the bomb
        slipped away from time,
escaping the roar and blast
        and cruel heat
                        that stopped the city.

In the turmoil of the bomb
the people—yes, the people—
        of Hiroshima
were swirled as in a witch's cauldron.
They sizzled and melted
        in that brew,
the day this tragic era was born.

FORGIVE ME, MOTHER

for Shoji Sawada

He stayed home from school that day
with a burning fever.

After the bomb, the young boy
awakened beneath the rubble of his room.

He could hear his mother's cries,
still trapped within the fallen house.

He struggled to free her, but he lacked
the strength.

A fire raged toward them,
and many people hurried past.

Frightened and dazed, they would not stop
to help him free his mother.

He could hear her voice from the rubble.
The voice was soft but firm.

"You must run and save yourself,"
she told him. "You must go."

"Forgive me," he said, bowing,
"Forgive me, Mother"

He did as his mother wished.
That was long ago, in 1945.

The boy has long been a man, a good man.
Yet he still runs from those flames.

POET FROM ANOTHER PLANET

for Robert Bly

You came from another planet
one that is bone dry
with more energy than mere earthlings.
Your imagination was primitive and boundless.

You hung a long red *serape*
with black designs over your shoulders.
It swirled as you danced and chanted,
danced and chanted.

Your words made no sense
but you uttered them
with such conviction
and danced with such awkward grace

that we were enchanted by your truths,
whatever they were,
and were ready to follow you anywhere,
even to distant stars—

the ones that can barely be seen
in the clear night sky,
the ones whose light
takes a million years

to reach us, the ones
that may have died long ago,
scattering their remains
throughout the universe.

We were young
but that does not explain it all.
You gave us the gift of freshness
and we embraced you

like tired, thirsty wanderers,
welcomed home at last.

DANCE OF HIROSHIMA

I watched you dance
the dance of Hiroshima,
your eyes filled with
a sorrow so deep
it opened your heart
and small birds flew away.

With faltering steps
you became a child,
a maiden, a mother,
a widow, a mourner.
You stumbled and fell,
you picked yourself up,
grew wings and flew away.

I watched you dance
your fear and anger,
your youth and magic.
I watched you rise
from the ashes, fly
with the wings of a crane
and float slowly back to Earth.

PROMISES OF PEACE

The last century, a monument to war,
keeps marching into the future.
Fathers don't know what to tell their sons,
but the dull leader knows:

> *Find the enemy and kill him.*

And *him* may be a mother or her sweet child.
Patriotic words always mean that someone soon
will die. It's carved in solemn stone.
The bombs don't calculate, they only

> *Seek the enemy to kill.*

There is no beauty in war, nor decency, nor
wisdom. There is only force and blind obedience.
Bombs fall, children die and generals are celebrated.
In the public square new names, new sacrifice.

> *Promises of peace give way to war.*

ASSASSIN

In the darkness,
like a thief,
you steal forth
again.

You raise
your coward's hand
and to his back
take aim.

Women wail
and grieve.
Men cry out
in pain.

To the martyrs
fallen,
now add the name
Rabin.

This holy land
makes claim
upon new blood,
new stain.

THAT WAS THEN, THIS IS NOW

"We had to destroy the village
to save it."
–An American Colonel

We had to destroy the village
the whole damn village
every last living soul
every thatched roof hut
every stick, every stone
to save it.

That was then.

We had to destroy the world
the whole damn world
every high rise
every thatched roof hut
every living thing
that walks, that crawls, that flies
that laughs, that sings, that cries
to save it.

This is now.

NEW YORK, APRIL 30, 2000

Twenty–five years ago America
lost its war in Vietnam.
I have reached the age
when I no longer want to hate

men like Johnson, McNamara, Nixon
or be disgusted by their napalm-dropping
high-altitude bombing, Agent Orange defoliating
body counting war in Vietnam.

In New York, it is a bright Sunday morning.
Women walk their dogs along the sidewalks.
Joggers run in place and then dart off.
One young woman retches in a wire trash bin.

In cement planter boxes, red tulips stand in rows
like small soldiers. Magnolias in full bloom
impress like cherry blossoms, their petals fluttering
slowly to the ground.

WORSE THAN THE WAR

Worse than the war, the endless, senseless war
Worse than the lies leading to the war

Worse than the countless deaths and injuries
Worse than hiding the coffins and not attending funerals

Worse than the flouting of international law
Worse than the torture at Abu Ghraib prison

Worse than the corruption of young soldiers
Worse than undermining our collective sense of decency

Worse than the arrogance, smugness and swagger
Worse than our loss of credibility in the world
Worse than the loss of our liberties

Worse than learning nothing from the past
Worse than destroying the future
Worse than the incredible stupidity of it all

Worse than all of these,
As if they were not enough for one war or country or lifetime,
Is the silence, the resounding silence, of good Americans.

A CONSPIRACY OF DECENCY

We will conspire to keep this blue dot floating and alive,
to keep the soldiers from gunning down the children,

to make the water clean and clear and plentiful,
to put food on everybody's table and hope in their hearts.

We will conspire to find new ways to say People matter.
This conspiracy will be bold.

Everyone will dance at wholly inappropriate times.
They will burst out singing non-patriotic songs.

And the not-so-secret password will be *Peace*.

ON PINOCHET'S ARREST

Buried with the Chinese clay soldiers, a message:
"One thousand autumns, ten thousand years."
What are we to make of it?

In cruelty, the potential for grandeur? Pinochet
thought he was not quite a dictator. Not quite.
He lasted longer than the disappeared.

Seventeen years of power, seventeen autumns.
But now he is nothing, less than nothing,
less even than Kissinger.

The courage of the disappeared remains, while
nothing much remains of Pinochet—
A few buildings, a foundation, some medals.

It is said that they dropped the disappeared
from planes into the ocean, their bellies split open
so that they would sink.

Imagine the sharks going after them.
As Pinochet went after Allende.
As Kissinger ripped into the guts of democracy.

Each autumn the leaves darken like blood.
Crisp leaves fall like dictators.
This autumn we celebrate Pinochet's humiliation.

THE DRUMS

They're beating on the drums again,
the drums, the drums.
They're calling out the young men again,
young men, young men.

They're training them to kill again,
with knives and guns,
with tanks and bombs.

They're sending them away again,
across the ocean
by ship, by plane.

They're acting up at home again,
the mothers, the mothers.
They don't want their sons to go again
to die, to die.

And now they're coming home again
in caskets wrapped in flags
with shrapnel in their backs,
with heroin in their veins.

And now they're coming home again
with snickers on their lips,
with medals on their chests.

They're blowing on the bugles now.
They're beating on the drums,
the drums, the drums.

IN TRUTH, WE ARE
BOMBING OURSELVES

Snails speak louder to truth
than our politicians speak to conscience,
and the voices of frogs are clearer yet than poets.

The truth which touches me across time and space
is risking all for life.

It flows in mother's milk,
echoes from the feet
of those who refused to be soldiers,
is carried on the backs of snails,
proclaimed in the voices of frogs
and knows no boundaries.

GOD RESPONDED WITH TEARS

The bomb dropped far slower than the speed of light.
It dropped at the speed of bombs.

From the ground it was a tiny silver speck
that separated from the silver plane.

The plane flew over Hiroshima and dropped the bomb
after the *All Clear* warning had sounded.

After 43 seconds, the slow falling bomb exploded
into mass at the speed of light squared.

Einstein called it energy. Everything lit up.
For a split-second people could see their own bones.

The pilot always believed he had done the right thing.
The President, too, never wavered from his belief

that he had done the right thing.
He thanked God for the bomb. Others did, too.

God responded with tears that fell far slower
than the speed of bombs.

They still have not reached Earth.

THE DEEP BOW OF A *HIBAKUSHA*

for Miyoko Matsubara

She bowed deeply. She bowed deeper than the oceans. She bowed from the top of Mt. Fuji to the bottom of the ocean. She bowed so deeply and so often that the winds blew hard.

The winds blew her whispered apologies and prayers across all the continents. But the winds whistled too loudly, and made it impossible to hear her apologies and prayers. The winds made the oceans crazy. The water in the oceans rose up in a wild molecular dance. The oceans threw themselves against the continents. The people were frightened. They ran screaming from the shores. They feared the white water and the whistling wind. They huddled together in dark places. They strained to hear the words in the wind.

In some places there were some people who thought they heard an apology. In other places there were people who thought they heard a prayer.

She bowed deeply. She bowed more deeply than anyone should bow.

A DANGEROUS FACE

It is a weak and fleshy face,
a face with furtive eyes
that snake along the ground, refusing
to rise and face forward.

He chews his words well,
mixing them with fire.
Words that dart like missiles
from the side of his malformed mouth.

It is a dangerous, deceitful face,
the face of a man with too many secrets.
It is the face of one who quietly orders
torturers to torture, assassins to strike.

It is the face *not* of a sniper,
but of one who orders snipers into action.
It is a face hidden behind a mask,
the face of one who savors lynchings.

It is the face of one who hides in dark bunkers
and shuns the brightness of the sun.
It is a frightened face, dull and without color,
the face of one consumed by power.

It is a weak and fleshy face,
a face with furtive eyes.
A face that falls hard and fast
like the blade of a guillotine.

FIRING SQUAD

Saddam Hussein is a bad man.
So let's line up the children of Iraq
and shoot them.

Saddam is a very bad man.
So let's line up the mothers of Iraq
and shoot them.

We know that Saddam is a bad man.
So let's line up all the old people of Iraq
and shoot them.

Saddam is a very bad man
and firing squads are old fashioned.
So let's just bomb Baghdad.

After we've bombed the Iraqis
with our "shock and awe" two-day plan
surely they will welcome us as liberators.

Surely the Iraqis will thank Allah
that they have been so fortunate
to have been bombed with such precision.

Surely they will recognize
that Saddam is a very bad man
and their oil is better in our hands.

Saddam Hussein is a very bad man.
So let's line up the children of Iraq
and shoot them.

WHEN THE BOMB BECAME OUR GOD

When the bomb became our god
we loved it far too much,
worshipping no other gods before it.

We thought ourselves great
and powerful, creators of worlds.

We turned toward infinity,
giving the bomb our very souls.

We looked to it for comfort,
to its smooth metallic grace.

When the bomb became our god
we lived in a constant state of war
that we called *peace*.

ONCE MEN COULD READ THE STARS

Once men could read the stars.
They knew many stories.
Once they knew how to greet bears,
but that was long ago.

Once athletes loved what they did,
more even than victory.
Once enemy was not a word,
not even a thought.

There is a longing for a simpler time,
before there were countries or flags.
But the longing is unspoken,
hidden just beyond our grasp.

Don't speak to me of riches.
Speak of simpler things.
Speak of broad dark skies
with too many stars to count.

REMEMBERING OURSELVES

Once we swam with incredible grace
in full, open oceans, restless and free.
Now we struggle against the parched harshness,
the sameness of ourselves.

Ships, stranded and abandoned,
are strange artifacts, at rest, at peace,
in the fierce, empty sunlight, but who
will find them? Who will worship them?

The centuries have been dry and hard,
but who would have thought that this
would be our end, to fade away
into endless desert?

The earth was once green and lush,
filled with life and wonder, but we formed
seas of soldiers and sailed away
so happily to war.

A SHOT RINGS OUT, A SOLDIER FALLS

"Bring 'em on."
–George W. Bush

Young Americans, soldiers, sentries, oceans from home
in the concrete jungles of Iraq, cradle of civilization,

dressed in desert camouflage, which hides nothing,
which announces, "I am a target," standing guard,

not knowing who is the enemy, but suspecting everyone,
wearing their helmets low on their foreheads, hands gripped

tightly on their weapons, feeling the nerves, ready to shoot,
not eager to kill, but ready, homesick, hearts pounding,

missing their sweethearts, knowing the president lies,
knowing the weapons of mass destruction are at home,

remembering Rumsfeld's smirk and Cheney's crooked mouth,
wanting only to go home, home from this dreary desert,

home from this place they don't belong, home
before they are shot or hit a mine or are bombed,
home before they die.

THE CHILDREN OF IRAQ HAVE NAMES

The children of Iraq have names.
They are not the nameless ones.

The children of Iraq have faces.
They are not the faceless ones.

The children of Iraq do not wear Saddam's face.
They each have their own face.

The children of Iraq have names.
They are not all called Saddam Hussein.

The children of Iraq have hearts.
They are not the heartless ones.

The children of Iraq have dreams.
They are not the dreamless ones.

The children of Iraq have hearts that pound.
They are not meant to be statistics of war.

The children of Iraq have smiles.
They are not the sullen ones.

The children of Iraq have twinkling eyes.
They are quick and lively with their laughter.

The children of Iraq have hopes.
They are not the hopeless ones.

The children of Iraq have fears.
They are not the fearless ones.

The children of Iraq have names.
Their names are not collateral damage.

What do you call the children of Iraq?
Call them Omar, Mohamed, Fahad.

Call them Marwa and Tiba.
Call them by their names.

UNHEALED WOUNDS OF HUMANITY

Auschwitz, Armenia,
Baghdad, Belau, Belfast,
Bethlehem, Bhopal, Biafra,
Bikini, Bosnia,
Cambodia, Chernobyl, Chiapas,
Dachau, Darfur, Dresden,
Eritrea, Ethiopia,
Guernica,
Hamburg, Hanoi, Hiroshima,
Iwo Jima, Jakarta,
Jenin, Jerusalem,
Kabul, Kandahar, Kashmir,
Kent State, Kosovo, Kuwait,
Manhattan, Midway, My Lai,
Nagasaki, Nanking, Normandy,
Okinawa, Rwanda,
Saigon, San Salvador, Sarajevo,
Sierra Leone, Sudan,
Tibet, Tienamen Square, East Timor,
Three Mile Island, Tokaimura,
Treblinka,
Wounded Knee, wounded hearts,
and the list goes on . . .

MOTHER'S DAY, 1969

Last night
we marched
in broken ranks
carrying candles
through the city
from the church
to the war memorial.

There is no peace memorial
in our city
and no one asks
why.

At the church
we prayed for peace.
Men spoke of peace—
the individual responsibility
of peace,
peace in words,
peace in action,
war in inaction.
We prayed.

We marched.
Gas station attendants stared.
We stared back, examining faces,
curious about souls,
faces and souls,
marching and staring.

Mothers waited at the war memorial.
Since early morning
they had been reading names
of Americans who died
in Vietnam
37,788 names
army names, navy names,
air force names, marine names.

Through the night
mothers read names
until they had read all
37,788 names
and when asked why
one replied,
"to arouse the public."

Arouse public minds faces names dead
public minds faces names dead
minds faces names dead
faces names dead
names dead.

One mother carried a sign
that said, "No more mother's sons,
not mine, not yours, not theirs."
The reading of names droned through the night.

Somewhere in Saigon Headquarters
new names were being added to the list.
Commanders were charting new plans,
pinning hopes of victory
to their battle maps.

It was lonely at the war memorial
holding those flickering candles
and listening to the names
on Mother's Day, 1969.

PASSING THROUGH KOKURA

The train pulls slowly into Kokura.
Towers belch thick smoke along its bay.
The city is compact, industrial, gray.

On a day destined to become infamous
for its crime and pain,
just three days after Hiroshima,

a US B-29
flew from Tinian Island
again.

The B-29, called *Bockscar*,
carried a single plutonium bomb,
a bomb meant to be dropped on Kokura.

But on that infamous day,
clouds covered Kokura, and
the bombardier couldn't see the ground.

The B-29 flew South, according to plan,
where the bombardier found
a break in the clouds.

He released the lethal cargo.
The bomb called *Fat Man* drifted down
and tens of thousands died that day
$$\text{in Nagasaki.}$$

The train speeds away from Kokura,
leaving behind its towers of belching smoke,
leaving behind this footnote in history.

YET ANOTHER FAREWELL

On the death of the 500th American soldier in Iraq

Let us lay the heavy black bag at your feet
while the tired buglers sound their dirge.

Let us lay the heavy black bag at your feet
like a terrible wreath.

If you nudge the sturdy bag with your right foot
nothing will happen.

If you kick the formless bag with your left foot
nothing will happen.

It will not respond, nor speak nor cry.

Will you circle the black bag cautiously
like a coyote?

Will you howl, break down in tears
or simply smirk?

SANCTUARY

A man stopped by our house with so little time for living that
he believed minutes were made of hours and night was made
for giving shelter to the day.

He came into our home and stared into the room that held his
youthful frame imprisoned in its space, and thinking of his
freedom lost, gloom spread across his face.

He played with our young child and took him to his breast
and felt his warm heart pounding in his tiny, tiny chest. He
remembered love he could not feel, the child he'd never see, the
woman waiting pregnant for the man he'd never be.

As images in a dream vanish in the night, one morning he was
gone, and where he'd been we found these words scribbled in a
note:

> *There are many ways, but the way is uncharted.*
> *There is ugliness too.* Lao Tzu.

WHAT SHALL WE CALL THE BOMB
DROPPED ON HIROSHIMA?

Shall we call it
Flash of White Light Maker or
Mushroom Cloud in Sky Maker?

Shall we call it
Terminator of War Bomb or
Incinerator of People Weapon?

Shall we call it
Secret Victory Weapon or
Dark Shadow Revealing Bomb?

Shall we call it
Rescuer of Young Soldiers Weapon or
Creator of Orphans Bomb?

Shall we call it
The Beginning of the End or
The End of the Beginning?

August 6, 1995

DECISION TO RESUME
BOMBING HANOI

Aides uncoil from their desks
and slither down dark corridors.
Approaching the President
their tongues flick red
from thin, dry lips.

The President hisses lowly,
approvingly,
slips to his belly,
glides toward his aides
until they entwine,
their rattles shivering.

Their tongues quiver menacingly
until the decision is made;
then slowly they slide apart.

AWAKENING

Waves of dawn
break against night,
slowly exposing
outlines of morning—
a cock crows, a dog howls,
green leaves in the sycamores,
darker green in the oaks,
twisted branches, uneven shapes
of our lives.

I twist and turn
trying for more sleep
in the stillness of dawn,
my mind darting
like a bee from one thought
to another—of taxes, speeches,
gatherings, of the day
that rolled by and the one
rolling in.

Three hours away in Washington
the President is helpless,
but not harmless.
He polishes his teeth, and practices
his famous smile.
Around him men and women
come and go, and speak of missiles
in their silos—while grain rots,
while dawn breaks, while Earth
races through space.

GUERNICA

Nazi Luftwaffe bombs fall
on a small Basque village.
It is market day.
The streets are jammed.

Nazis bomb and strafe.
Planes dive, machine guns fire.
The young Luftwaffe pilots
find the marketplace.

Villagers and peasants
run for their lives
as death blurts from the sky.
Seventeen hundred murdered and maimed.

Picasso shares his human outrage
in his unforgettable *Guernica,*
the Guernica of agonizing death.
Fallen man, fallen horse.

Bland bureaucrats may try to hide
this Guernica
to protect the shameless ones
who thunder for more war.

But Guernica cannot so easily
be put aside: Cover *Guernica*
and its power breaks through.
Starker, stronger, truer.

Symbol of wars horrors:
Screams of agony and death.
For those who would make war
Guernica was painted for you.

ROBERT MCNAMARA – 1995

Bearing the Burden of the Body Count

Your *mea culpa* took courage.
Not the sort of thing
McGeorge Bundy would do.

You broke the code of silence.

Your silence was a death sentence
to young Americans—
to young men who believed
        in America.

Your silence was a death sentence
to millions of Vietnamese.

Finally you speak out,
        with blood on your lips.

You are old.
I try to forgive you.
It isn't easy.

I can't forget
        your arrogance.
I can't forget
        the body counts

night after night after night.

WHAT IS HOLY

What is holy is not to walk on water.
What is holy is to walk on earth
 one step at a time.

What is holy is not silence.
It is the sound of wind through the leaves,
the sound of birds, of breathing, of voice.

What is holy is not purple robes.
What is holy is what is natural,
naked and unadorned.

What is holy is truth, simple truth,
and the willingness to seek it and speak it.
What is holy is not a cause, not an "ism."

What is holy are our connections to one another.

MEETING EINSTEIN IN MY GARDEN ON THE 50ᵀᴴ ANNIVERSARY OF HIROSHIMA

It is the fiftieth anniversary of the bombing of Hiroshima, and I have been sleeping in the garden under the shade of an oak tree. A gray cat with pointed ears, Kioni, is curled next to me, and the hummingbirds are attacking a feeder and occasionally each other. The light is filtered through the oak.

When I wake up I see the cat and the hummingbirds in the dappled afternoon light. One thing is unusual, though. Albert Einstein is sitting across from me wearing a rumpled gray sweatshirt that says, "Beat Army." A great mane of white hair surrounds his angelic face. He seems lost in thought and has a puzzled expression on his brow.

I am hesitant to say anything and interrupt his concentration. As I watch Einstein, his eyes closed in deep thought, I think it is extraordinary that he should be here on this day. Looking at him, I think about the mysterious ways in which good and evil mix in our lives, that someone with Einstein's purity of being should have understood mysteries of nature that gave rise to making atomic weapons. I remember reading what Einstein had said when he learned of the use of the bomb on Hiroshima, "I could burn my fingers that I wrote that first letter to Roosevelt."

He opens his eyes and smiles, a soft, angelic smile. "Fifty years," he says, "I am thankful each day those bombs are not used again." His voice has a charming melody, like flowing water. "One thing is certain," he continues, "the genie *can* be put back in the bottle. Just reverse my formula. Mass before energy. Thought before bombs. That's the key. And don't ever give up."

The cat points his ears as Einstein talks. The hummingbirds whiz past him. I wonder why he is telling me this. As I think this, he responds, "I might as well tell you as anyone. I just felt like talking, but I've been here too long. I must go." With that, he vanishes. Just like that.

Kioni nuzzles against me. The hummingbirds dart past. The dappled sunlight falls across the garden. It is as though Einstein had never been here.

August 6, 1995

BY GOVERNMENT ORDER
NOT SEEING IS BELIEVING

Photographs
of the destruction,
the maiming and suffering,
the death and dying,
were banned by order
of our government
from reaching
our people.

With photographs
of the children,
the mothers,
the dead and dying,
the suffering,
it would have been harder,
much harder,
to celebrate *the bomb*.

Without photographs
we could picture
the war ending cleanly,
the bomb exploding gently,
over a soulless city,
inhabited only
by *the enemy*.

Fifty years later
we still prefer to see
a shining *Enola Gay*
with its crew of young airmen
to photographs
of Hiroshima
at 8:15 a.m.
after the clock froze.

ON BECOMING DEATH

"Now I am become death, the destroyer of worlds."
–Bhagavad Gita

When Oppenheimer thought, "Now *I am* become death," did he mean, "Now *we have* become death? Was Oppenheimer thinking about himself or all of us?

From Alamogordo to Hiroshima took exactly three weeks. On August 6th, Oppenheimer again became death. So did Groves, Stimson and Byrnes. So did Truman. So did a hundred thousand that day in Hiroshima. And so did America.

"This is the greatest thing in history," Truman said. He didn't think *he'd* become death *that* day. We Americans know how to win. Truman was a winner, a *destroyer of worlds*. Three days later, Truman and his military boys did it again at Nagasaki.

Sometime later, Oppenheimer visited Truman. "I have blood on my hands," Oppenheimer said. Truman didn't like those words.

Blood? What blood? When Oppenheimer left, Truman said, "Don't ever let him in here again."

That August of '45 Truman and his military boys *destroyed* a few worlds. They never learned that among the worlds they destroyed was *their* own.

CROSSING THE BOUNDARY
OF ACADEMIC TOLERANCE

for Steve Stevens

You mixed metaphors,
expressed original ideas
and neglected to use footnotes.

You hiked through seven valleys
of wildness, asked questions
for which there were no answers.

You lived on the North side
of reality and cried out with pain
when the Earth suffered.

You left the classroom
and searched for decency.
That might have been all right

but when you found it
you brought it back.
What does it all mean?

It means you will never be one of them.
It means you will never have tenure.
It means that your soul is still intact.

LOOKING BACK ON SEPTEMBER 11TH

Each rising of the sun begins a day of awe, destined
to bring shock to those who can be shocked.

This day began in sunlight and, like other days,
soon fell beneath death's shadow.

The darkness crossed Manhattan and the globe,
the crashing planes, tall towers bursting into flame.

The hurtling steel into steel and glass endlessly played
on the nightly news until imprinted on our brains.

People lurching from the burning towers, plunging
like shot geese to the startled earth beneath.

But such death is not extraordinary in our world of grief,
born anew each brief and sunlit day.

White flowers grow from bloodstained streets
and rain falls gently, gently in defiance, not defeat.

ROAD MARKERS

We keep passing road markers
on the long, curved trail of death in Iraq.

There were one hundred thirty-eight dead American soldiers
when Bush, impersonating a combat pilot,
proclaimed: *Mission Accomplished.*

Then it was two hundred, then three, four, five hundred.
Now we have passed the nine hundred marker
on the bitter trail of death.

Are we safer? Do they hate us less?
Perhaps this doesn't happen until we pass a thousand,
or perhaps two or three or ten thousand.

Or perhaps not until as many Americans have died
as Iraqis we have killed.
Perhaps they will never hate us less.

Nor will we ever be safer
while we are dropping bombs on Iraqis, or Iranians,
or North Koreans. Anyone.

What was it we accomplished so early on the trail of death?
And didn't Bush look dashing all dressed up for war?

TODAY IS NOT
A GOOD DAY FOR WAR

Today is not a good day for war,
Not when the sun is shining,
And leaves are trembling in the breeze.

Today is not a good day for bombs to fall,
Not when clouds hang on the horizon
And drift above the sea.

Today is not a good day for young men to die,
Not when they have so many dreams
And so much still to do.

Today is not a good day to send missiles flying,
Not when the fog rolls in
And the rain is falling hard.

Today is not a good day for launching attacks,
Not when families gather
And hold on to one another.

Today is not a good day for collateral damage,
Not when children are restless
Daydreaming of frogs and creeks.

Today is not a good day for war,
Not when birds are soaring,
Filling the sky with grace.

No matter what they tell us about *the other*,
Nor how bold their patriotic calls,
Today is not a good day for war.

EARLY MORNING AT THE EPICENTER

Nagasaki, November 18, 2002

A chill is in the air this November morning.
Orange and yellow leaves tumble
across neatly laid red bricks.

On nearby grass, groundskeepers, old men,
rake the leaves into piles and gather them.
It is a gray morning, quiet and cold.

The epicenter of the crime is marked
by a simple black monolith,
pointing skyward.

Five hundred meters above,
the atomic bomb called *Fat Man*
shuddered and awakened.

At the base of the monolith are flowers,
Signs that the dead are not forgotten,
their dreams still with the living, vibrant

as the colorful folded cranes hanging nearby
in tightly bunched clusters.

HIBAKUSHA STILL LIVE ON EARTH

Hibakusha
still live
on earth

their soft
voices
of forgiveness

testimony
to our human
spirit

they bow deep
thanking us
for listening

to their
sad and painful
stories

Someday
the last *hibakusha*
will take

a last breath
and be
no more

but their pain
and their stories
will live on

HIBAKUSHA DO NOT JUST HAPPEN

For every *hibakusha*
there is a pilot.

For every *hibakusha*
there is a planner.

For every *hibakusha*
there is a bombardier.

For every *hibakusha*
there is a bomb designer.

For every *hibakusha*
there is a missile maker.

For every *hibakusha*
there is a missileer.

For every *hibakusha*
there is a targeter.

For every *hibakusha*
there is a commander.

For every *hibakusha*
there is a button pusher.

For every *hibakusha*
many must contribute.

For every *hibakusha*
many must obey.

For every *hibakusha*
many must be silent.

WILD STARS AND NEGLECTED ANNIVERSARIES

"What has happened to the soul of the destroying nation is yet too early to see. Forces of nature act in a mysterious manner."
–Gandhi

The 59th anniversary of the atomic bombing of Hiroshima
has come and gone with almost no notice in America.

In this country, we are still flying high above the bomb,
making hard, sharp turns to evade responsibility.

On the 59th anniversary of the atomic bombing of Nagasaki
America is still fighting in distant lands.

In Najaf, US troops surround the holy Shrine of Imam Ali,
as though the Crusades never ended.

Americans are too busy to imagine being beneath the bomb.
That is for others less fortunate to imagine.

Fifty-nine years is hardly a tick on the geological clock,
one that has witnessed far too many wars and atrocities.

One day we will wonder what happened to the brightness,
to all the wild stars and neglected anniversaries.

THE BELLS OF NAGASAKI

The bells of Nagasaki
ring for those who suffered
and those who suffer still.

They draw old women to them
and young couples
wth love-glazed eyes.

They draw the children to them,
small children walking awkwardly
toward the epicenter.

The Bells of Nagasaki,
elusive as a flowing stream,
ring for each of us.
They ring like falling leaves.

EINSTEIN'S REGRET

Einstein's regret ran deep
Like the pools of sorrow
That were his eyes.

His mind could see things
That others could not,
The bending of light,

The slowing of time,
Relationships of trains passing
In the night, and power,

Dormant and asleep,
That could be awakened,
But who would dare?

He saw patterns
In snowflakes and stars,
Unimaginable simplicity

To make one weep with joy.

When the shadow of Hitler
Spread across Europe
What was Einstein to do

But what he did?
His regret ran deep, deeper
Than the deep pools of sorrow

That were his eyes.

WHEN THE DRAFT COMES BACK

Questions for young Americans

When the draft comes back,
will you close your books, march to the light of the moon,
and learn to love your rifle as a favored friend?

Will you set aside your studies and your dreams
for a sabbatical of suspended reason,
and a long vacation from your conscience?

Will you learn new ways to distance yourself from life and love,
and hate the enemy, those ragged, rock-throwing throngs
who speak other languages, worship other gods,
and live in barren places?

When the draft comes back, will you polish your boots,
put on camouflage, snap to attention, and say, Yes Sir,
when ordered to kill?

Or, will you stand your ground, look your leaders in their eyes
tell them that you have more and better things to do
but when they lead the way themselves to war,
you'll consider going, too?

AN IMPROBABLE GARDEN

Where I go, sad city, you go with me.
You are not worldly like Paris or Rome,
but neither am I.
You are not a city of snow-capped peaks,
nor one with the calm sea wrapped around you.
These wonders do not change the soul.
You are not New York, nor Delhi, nor Rio
with their milling throngs and excitement.
Such noise and light and busy-ness
are too ephemeral for you.

Your heritage is honorable. That counts
for something. After your tragedy
you showed the depth of your spirit.
You clawed your own earth
until the plants slowly came back.
You are a city built on the ashes of war,
a city where a flower is still a miracle.
You are a city with the courage
to return from the dead.
Your people bow deeply and smile
their sorrowful smiles.

Hiroshima, sad city, I give you
the intensity of my solitude.
I give you the drum beat of my heart.
I carry you with me in the hope
that from your spirit a better world
may one day sprout and blossom.
I give you the salt of my tears
to mix with your grief and promise.
Hiroshima, you are an improbable garden
and I, an even more improbable gardener.

ON BECOMING HUMAN

To be human is to recognize the cultural perspectives that bind us to tribe, sect, religion, or nation, and to rise above them. It is to feel the pain of the dispossessed, the downtrodden, the refugee, the starving child, the slave, the victim.

To be human is to break the ties of cultural conformity and group-think, and to use one's own mind. It is to recognize good and evil, and to choose good. It is to consider with the heart. It is to act with conscience.

To be human is to be courageous. It is to choose the path of compassion. It is to sacrifice for what is just. It is to break the silence. It is to be an unrelenting advocate of human decency and human dignity.

To be human is to breathe with the rhythm of life, and to recognize our kinship with all forms of life. It is to appreciate every drop of water. It is to feel the warmth of the sun, and to marvel at the beauty and expanse of the night sky. It is to stand in awe of who we are and where we live. It is to see the Earth with the eyes of an astronaut.

To be human is to be aware of our dependence upon the whole of the universe, and of the miracle that we are. It is to open our eyes to the simple and extraordinary beauty that is all about us. It is to live with deep respect for the sacred gift of life. It is to love.

To be human is to seek to find ourselves behind our names. It is to explore the depths and boundaries of our existence. It is to learn from those that have preceded us, and act with due concern for those who will follow us.

To be human is to plant the seeds of peace, and nurture them. It is to find peace and make peace. It is to help mend the web of life. It is to be a healer of the planet.

To be human is to say an unconditional No to warfare, and particularly to all weapons of mass destruction. It is to take a firm stand against all who profit from warfare and its preparation.

To be human is not always to succeed, but it is always to learn. It is to move forward despite the obstacles.

We are all born with the potential to become fully human. How we choose to live will be the measure of our humanness. Civilization does not assure our civility. Nor does being born into the human species assure our humanity. We must each find our own path to becoming human.

FIFTY-ONE REASONS FOR HOPE

1. Each new dawn.
2. The miracle of birth.
3. Our capacity to love.
4. The courage of nonviolence.
5. Gandhi, King and Mandela.
6. The night sky.
7. Spring.
8. Flowers and bees.
9. The arc of justice.
10. Whistleblowers.
11. Butterflies.
12. The full moon.
13. Teachers.
14. Simple wisdom.
15. Dogs and cats.
16. Friendship.
17. Our ability to reflect.
18. Our capacity for joy.
19. The Dalai Lama, Desmond Tutu and Oscar Romero.
20. The gift of conscience.
21. Human rights and responsibilities.
22. Our capacity to nurture.
23. The ascendancy of women.
24. Innocence.
25. Our capacity to change.
26. Mozart, Beethoven and Chopin.
27. The internet.
28. War resisters.
29. Everyday heroes.

30. Lions, tigers, bears, elephants and giraffes.
31. Conscientious objectors.
32. Tolstoy, Twain and Vonnegut.
33. Wilderness.
34. Our water planet.
35. Solar energy.
36. Picasso, Matisse and Miro.
37. World citizens.
38. Life.
39. The survivors of Hiroshima and Nagasaki.
40. The King of Hearts.
41. Rain.
42. Sunshine.
43. Pablo Neruda.
44. Grandchildren.
45. Mountains.
46. Sunflowers.
47. The Principles of Nuremberg.
48. A child's smile.
49. Dolphins.
50. Wildflowers.
51. Our ability to choose hope.

SADAKO AND THE SHAKUHACHI

We remember Hiroshima not for the past, but for the future. We remember Hiroshima so that its past will not become our future. Hiroshima is best remembered with the plaintive sounds of the bamboo flute, the Shakuhachi. It conjures up the devastation, the destruction, the encompassing emptiness of that day. The Shakuhachi reveals the tear in the fabric of humanity that was ripped open by the bomb.

Nuclear weapons are not weapons at all. They are a symbol of an imploding human spirit. They are a fire that consumes the crisp air of decency. They are a crossroads where science joined hands with evil and apathy. They are a triumph of academic certainty wrapped in the convoluted lie of deterrence. They are Einstein's regret. They are many things, but not weapons – not instruments of war, but of genocide and perhaps of omnicide.

Those who gather to retell and listen to the story of Hiroshima and of Sadako are a community, a community committed to a human future. We may not know one another, but we are a community. And we are part of a greater community gathered throughout the world to commemorate this day, seeking to turn Hiroshima to Hope.

If we succeed, Sadako of a thousand cranes will be remembered by new generations. She will be remembered long after the names and spirits of those who made and used the bomb will have faded into the haunting sounds of the Shakuhachi.

YOU ARE NOT ONE BUT MANY

Remembering Martin Luther King, Jr.

Your deep voice still hangs in the air,
melting the cowardly silence.
You are the one standing solidly there
looking straight in the face of violence.

You are the one who dreams
that this nation will honor its creed.
You are the one who steps forward.
You are the one to bleed.

You are not one but many
unwilling to cower or crawl.
You are the one who will take no less
than a world that is just for all.

DREAMS

"If you can dream it, you can do it."
–Walt Disney

Of course, such words may inspire,
but can dreams really be unlocked?

If you can dream the wind,
can you really make the leaves tremble?

If you can dream the rain,
can you really soak the parched earth or make
the rivers swell and rush to the sea?

If you can dream the moon,
can you really move the tides
and cast your shadow on the earth?

If you can dream peace,
can you make young men, boys really,
disobey the generals and lay down their arms?

Yes, it's unlikely, but someone has to dream
of making the leaves tremble, the rivers swell,
the tides move, and the young men

find better uses for their only lives.

ADVICE TO GRADUATES

Always remember this:
You are a miracle
made up of dancing atoms
that can talk and sing,
listen and remember, and laugh,
at times even at yourself.

You are a miracle
whose atoms existed before time.
Born of the Big Bang, you are connected
to everything—to mountains and oceans,
To the winds and wilderness, to the creatures
of the sea and air and land.
You are a member of the human family.

You are a miracle, entirely unique.
There has never been another
with your combination of talents, dreams,
desires and hopes. You can create.
You are capable of love and compassion.

You are a miracle.
You are a gift of creation to itself.
You are here for a purpose, which you must find.
Your presence here is sacred – and you will
change the world.

ACKNOWLEDGMENTS

This book is the realization of a long-time dream. It is a dream that would not have been possible without the support of my wife Carolee, who has stood by my side as I have fought against war and the mind-sets and worldviews that sustain it. Nor could it have happened without the support of my colleagues at the Nuclear Age Peace Foundation.

I want to express my gratitude to poet Perie Longo, who believed that this collection of poems should become a book and who gave me encouragement and much needed help in making this book a reality. I want to acknowledge with appreciation the strong support I received for this project from Gerry Spence, Richard Falk and Virginia Castagnola-Hunter.

I want to thank Kathleen Baushke for her saintly patience and her skill in typesetting and design. I also want to thank Bob Bason at Capra Press for giving this project his blessing and support.

Many of the poems in this volume have been incorporated in speeches that I have given throughout the world, and some of them have appeared previously in print. *On Becoming Human* first appeared in **What Does It Mean to Be Human?**, compiled and edited by Frederick Franck, Janis Roze and Richard Connolly (New York: St Martin's Press, 2000). It also appeared, along with *Unhealed Wounds of Humanity* and *The Deep Bow of a Hibakusha* in **Hope in a Dark Time**, edited by David Krieger (Santa Barbara: Capra Press, 2003). *Peace Is…*, *Dance of Hiroshima* and *The Young Men with the Guns* appeared in **The Poetry of Peace**, edited by David Krieger (Santa Barbara: Capra Press, 2003).

The following poems appeared in **The Legal Studies Forum** (Volume XXVIII, No.1 & 2): *Today is Not a Good Day for War*; *War Is Too Easy*; *God Responded with Tears*; *Passing through Kokura*; *Hibakusha Still Live on Earth*; *Hiroshima Dreams*; *Einstein's Regret*; *Guernica*; *Unhealed Wounds of Humanity*; and *A Short History Lesson: 1945*. *The Drums* appeared in **The Humanist** (Nov./Dec. 2002:6). *When the Bomb Became Our God* appeared in **Locusts & Wild Honey** (2000:7). Other poems in this volume have appeared on the web sites: *Wagingpeace.org, Poetsagainstthewar.org, Poetryinwartime.org, Counterpunch.org and Web-tracks.org.*

NUCLEAR AGE PEACE FOUNDATION

The Nuclear Age Peace Foundation is a non-profit, non-partisan international organization on the Roster in consultative status to the United Nations Economic and Social Council. Founded in 1982, the Foundation is a catalyst in enhancing global security by initiating and supporting efforts to reduce nuclear dangers; strengthen international law and institutions; and inspire and empower a new generation of peace leaders.

Vision: A world at peace, free of the threat of war and free of weapons of mass destruction.

Mission: To advance initiatives to eliminate the nuclear weapons threat to all life, to foster the global rule of law, and to build an enduring legacy of peace through education and advocacy.

Projects: Information on Foundation projects, including the annual Barbara Mandigo Kelly Peace Poetry Awards, can be found online at www.wagingpeace.org.

Nuclear Age Peace Foundation
PMB 121, 1187 Coast Village Road, Suite 1
Santa Barbara, CA 93108-2794

HOPE IN A DARK TIME
Reflections on Humanity's Future

Edited by David Krieger

Foreword by Archbishop Desmond Tutu

"The message of this important book is that hope matters. Hope is not only the light that can be found at the end of the tunnel. It is also the light, faint and flickering though it may be, that can help us navigate the darkness of our times."
                –Archbishop Desmond Tutu, from his Foreword

"This book is an invitation to hope and action. It is an invitation to set aside the obstacles to action, to choose peace and to wage peace. It is an invitation to help shape humanity's future."
                        –David Krieger, from his Introduction

THE POETRY OF PEACE

Edited by David Krieger

Foreword by Terry Tempest Williams

"May we read each one of these poems as a prayer. May we find inspiration in their courage to speak on behalf of peace."

–Terry Tempest Williams, from her Foreword

"In these poems one finds a burning desire to do more to heal wounded spirits and our wounded earth. These poems combine the mystery of creativity with a longing for peace."

–David Krieger, from his Introduction

Capra ♈ Press
Memorable Books Since 1969
Santa Barbara
155 Canon View Road
Santa Barbara, CA 93108
(805) 969-0203
www.caprapress.com

ABOUT CAPRA PRESS

Capra Press was founded in 1969 by the late Noel Young. Among its authors have been Henry Miller, Ross Macdonald, Margaret Millar, Edward Abbey, Anais Nin, Raymond Carver, Ray Bradbury and Lawrence Durrell. It is in this tradition that we present the new Capra: literary and mystery fiction, lifestyle and city books. Contact us.
We welcome your comments.

Robert E. Bason, Publisher

CAPRA ♈ PRESS
155 Canon View Road, Santa Barbara, CA 93108
(805) 969-0203
www.caprapress.com

Two thousand two hundred trade paperback copies of *Today Is Not a Good Day for War* were printed by Capra Press in January 2005. One hundred copies have been numbered and signed by the author. Twenty-six copies in slipcases were also lettered and signed.